Cottonmouth

COTTONMOUTH

Poems by

Miya Coleman

Button Publishing Inc.
Minneapolis
2024

COTTONMOUTH
POETRY
AUTHOR: Miya Coleman
COVER DESIGN: Talisa Almonte

Published by Button Poetry
Minneapolis, MN 55418 | http://www.buttonpoetry.com

Manufactured in the United States of America
PRINT ISBN: 978-1-63834-299-1
EBOOK ISBN: 978-1-63834-297-7
AUDIOBOOK ISBN: 978-1-63834-296-0

First printing

This collection is dedicated gracious to my Mother

if I sprout, you are soil
the first seed, a drop of dew, gentle heat
if I fly, you are wings
steady wind, hive, and sweet honey
if I do, you are
all you are, I pray to be

Contents

PART I:
GRANNY GOT ROACHES

Granny got roaches and she's had them for a while now.

I watch them crawl on the ceiling like they pay rent, infiltrating bathroom crevices until they become the baseboards she couldn't afford when she and Granddaddy bought the house back in 1970.

Granny got a lot of roaches.

But we still eat at her house on Thanksgiving, and let her spoon-feed us for Christmas because Granddaddy says:

At some point, we was all insects infecting this planet.

THE MEEKS' INHERITANCE

Ain't no heaven or hell
for a roach on the stove
the rich call the exterminator
like I ain't got no rights
I know adam, eve, and apple
pretend I wasn't first
to take a bite.

Dream in mules and acres
of inheriting earth and sea
of toil not a purposeful plan
of covenants all fulfilling.

I know what it's like

to be but a simile to poverty

to be an intruder on promised land

to ask for what you're owed
and to be granted captivity.

WATER MOCCASIN

wade knee deep in liquid earth. green-black creek
squished between bare toes, digging for treasure in a gentle
current, gliding to a screen door with a life trapped between palm
and dirty fingernails—

uncles lean in drowsy lawn chairs, legs bent under a
once-white folding table, hinges shivering under the slam of
dominoes, dust rising up
from middle crevice, the color of daddy's knuckles. he
funnel fresh greens from simmering pot to paper plate to plastic
fork, slurping amongst shuffling blocks, chin
dripping a color liquid that resemble the creek's stomach.
i sit next to the commotion on cracked cement birthing dandelion
bouquets from its fractures, dirt-stained
feet brushing each other, knees splayed like butterfly wings—

startled, suddenly
by a summer-time insect's thirst, i release my grip and the
borrowed life hops away from me toward home. i remain in place
and count to ten—

i chase it past the garage, through the unmowed grass,
around the makeshift fire pit made of rocks and wire, and the
dying pear tree, bark engulfing a rusted swing bolted
to one outstretched limb. halfway through the meadow, i
halt. a curved spine creeps forward and rises like the blades of
earth it hides in, bending as they do
toward the sun, sensing heat and hissing at approaching
appendages, coiled and trigger ready, stomach churning
emptiness—

body slicing through wind, bare feet calloused and numb
to rugged earth carry me in the opposite direction, towards
home, leaving the amphibian as sacrifice—

under domesticated grass and safety, i collapse between
a rotting pear, open and spilling, and a limp, hollow film.
unclaimed, twisted around
        itself, a pale new treasure. the story of a creature
different than it was then. when filled with blood and bone and
muscle, forgotten
        identity outlined in the ridges of shed skin, remembered
as something with breath—

        before becoming captive to pirating hands, cornbread and
salt pork sizzling amongst hot oil make their way past the garage,
around the fire pit, place themselves
        in the pear tree's palms, calls *come home*,
        and the discarded body is left to be alive to the next
creature's sense it touches.

THE ORIGIN OF EBONICS, PART 1

a language first rolled up in west africa
as a leaf pressed to slave lips, lungs
hungry for final syllables & deep
inhalation while a king-led ship
kisses the coast of ocean-side province

white defined before a turning century
only as exhaled clouds, as balmy
breath that could palm read,
as purity, as a circulating speech
self-evident to those conversing

as senegal sits on familiar soil
legs twisted, fingers & lips synced
in studied motion, as togo singing
a burnt-lipped melody to guinea,
gambia rotating earth into cocoon
passed from ghana to benin, two
puffs, clockwise again, a vernacular
sent to mali, fingertips that sustain
medicinal healing long after
the turning of leaves

dialects as molded terracotta,
malleable strains grown from
heat, rain, & open fire, as
free-verse embellishment,
a past narrative hardened,
amplified, passed on again

perhaps a blue-black nighttime
sky lays uninterrupted on skin as
invocation scribbled in venous
ink, requesting the gods forgive
us our trespasses & all of our
trespassers' sins

SINCERELY, THE RAINFOREST

I, too, know a world warmer.

Gripped lungs close to collapse.
Smelled rot & felt familiar.
Been cut down by chainsaw
& branded by fire, my body
at the disposal of a stranger.

I, too, been dug up at the root.

Screamed for help in the wrong
tongue. Been fallen, injured in
my own home, classified hysteric
& told I never made a sound.

I, too, been domesticated.

Evolved adjacent to my planter.
Told to grow rich fruit & had
my seeds sold for profit.

Like you, I compare myself to them.

How I develop at a slower rate
yet die by exponent.

LIKE NATURE

she is not addressed properly
and so, remains silent

she knows that smoke is rarely seen
before caressing the highest cloud

the trees bore from her belly
breastfeeding hungry lungs will be

axed, opened, and autopsied until all
heavy breathers are under-oxygenated

her hands, alone gifting sustenance, bitten
soft enough to be claimed as a simple kiss

and screaming winds, harmonious
until the deepest sleepers lose rest

when bleeding wounds wrapped in loose
bandage begin to consider infection

once her absence takes effect

will her children, then, attempt
to decelerate her approaching death?

PART II:
THE ROACHES THAT STAY

At seven, I beg Granny to fill the bathtub higher, promising I will not drown if the water reaches my ribs. She fills it just as far as her anxiety allows and not any further, not even an inch.

Granny takes my hand and helps me climb out of the shallow basin, dries my body with one of the good towels, the soft yellow one with no holes in it, then covers me from head to toe in Vaseline. I put on my pajamas. Granny tucks me in. She scratches my back until there is enough space between my blinks for her to exit.

Granny says: I love you.

I say: I love you, too.

And Granny vanishes to the room she shares with a man and his roaches, moving in soft limps like her bones are aching much worse than they did yesterday . . . even though she didn't think it could get any more painful than it was yesterday.

I wonder how many roaches follow her out. I wonder how many choose to stay under the covers with me.

2013

She walks, shoelaces dragging like chalk
tracing trope against concrete
ears plugged with ivory headphones
music harmonized with self-critique.

She stands, natural hair bud-length
pubescent and blooming
concealed by artificial curls
resting straight-down center back.

She dreams, of bleach-stained skin
never once touched by pigment
for the luminescence of white
of a blue-eyed body untainted.

Somehow, she never notices pale peers
mimicking her moves from a distance
with fine hair plaited tightly to scalp
and colorless complexions spray painted.

PROPAGANDA'S CURSE

Looking down myself while a showerhead hoses me clean. Eight hours spent under white-hot sun. The water rolling into the shower drain is the color of mud or mold or both. After soap and pressure, the water runs clear. I am still dyed a hue of dirt. My bathtub mocks me in shiny porcelain. When rings form around its center, my mother tells me to scrub it clean. Not done until we exist on two opposite ends of a spectrum again. The salon smells like powder and singe. Toya reminds me the relaxer will burn. It is noxious by necessity. Must be strong enough to put an afro on its back. We hold fire to my scalp for ten minutes. I welcome this pain like the first breath after a deep dive. After all, pain is what beauty is.

I said all that to say:

> If I could convince my skin to turn white, the same way Toya's ointment converts kinks to straight, I'd bathe in it until this blackness burns and blanches, until it has no choice but to run away.

◆ ◇ ◆

Looking down myself as a pretty girl with wings walks down a never-ending runway. I hear these women dip cotton balls in orange juice to stay thin. After three weeks, I still possess the same proportions. My homecoming dress mocks me; this is not the body it envisioned covering. I interrupt the fabric's descent, pushing it outward with an oversized lower body. On TV, gowns fall off angels' shoulders and drop evenly down legs. Imagine water streaming from a faucet. I must minimize myself to find beauty. Beauty is petite. Sarah Baartman spends years in a European freak show. Paraded around while colonizers gawk at her shape. Othered due to a body that resembles the one I am dissecting in the mirror currently. I have never been able to get this silhouette to change.

I said all that to say:

> If I could actually convince my body to morph to model, the same way a flatter figure might've saved Baartman from her fate, I'd eat cotton balls until there's none left to pick, until my ancestors rise from their graves, forced to collect the cotton I regurgitate.

LOST

I heard cardio makes you lose weight.
So every day for five months
I walked as far as I could.

But now, I am miles from home
and don't know where I am.

DOUBLE TAP DOPAMINE

I posted only
My failures on Instagram
Strangers privately messaged
Asking what was wrong
As if I had not just told them.

I posted only
My successes on Instagram
Strangers commented publicly
Praising my amazing life
As if they truly knew enough

To assign my reality an
adjective.

YOU SOUND WHITE

been bitter before
been ghost
pepper
dry swallow
scream covered
in milk,
sour nose on
expiration day
oreo over-dipped,
not even a
footnote
in a pretty white
boy's storybook.

in high school
i snapped,
imagine:
quick bite,
clamp!
of pearly white
teeth,
entire self
a rubber band
echo
bounced off
glacier face,
my cries a
high-pitched
beluga,

mute to most.

legs angled
90 degrees
cliff-hanging
above
churning
whitecaps,
frothy from
a birds-eye,
brimming
over jagged
limestone
threatening
to halt a
swan dive.

i remember
when granny
dragged a wet
rag across my
face because
i soiled
the mattress
again,
clumsy center
stain, i crack
like always

a thin eggshell,
imagine:
yolk diffusing
on virgin linen
i was 10 then
cousins confused
how i still can't
hold my piss,
truth is,
i been
holding it in
i *been*
holding it in
no option
to sound angry,
real angry
'cus my words
come out
lined white like
a cottonmouth
jaw, unhinged
always on
defense,
never real
threatening
though.

PART III:
IGNORANCE AS BLISS

We still eat at Granny's house even though she got roaches because, even though she got roaches, she keeps the heat on heavy. Lays on warmth like reunion hugs with love so thick I think I understand why the roaches won't ever leave. She says it's been so long that she doesn't notice them anymore, as if she bought black paint and crafted polka dots on the walls in her sleep.

Granny cannot smell the sooty stench of her House. Does not notice once-white walls now stained the color of piss. She forgot how obvious addiction is to those unacquainted with it.

She places symbols of White Jesus around her, on side tables, and sutured to her House's skin. Granny does not discern any irony in promising devotion to a white man, while living on the discarded half of a segregated city, paying taxes to keep the colorless side of its red line clean. Then there is Grandaddy, who vowed to love and cherish Granny until death do they part, though the treatment she receives now is nothing close to promises made at the altar.

There are three ways to view Granny's ignorance. It is either willing, inherent, or conditioned. It could be all three, but truthfully, I don't know what the answer is yet. Perhaps White Jesus made Granny this way on purpose; it is only fair to also offer the deprived a method to bliss.

Granny says: Carl, a roach is on your pork chop.

Granddaddy says: Betty if you don't shut up, I swear to God.

And Granny says nothing.

The rest of us study our plates with eyes wide, swatting at each intruder that tries to take a bite before we say Amen.

NOW LET ME RISE—A SLAVE SONG

Refrain

I will rise,
I will rise,
Now let me fly way up high,
To see de Promise Land.

1. Work all day stuck up in this field,
   Tell the sky I don' like it here.
   Not meant for work, but work I know,
   Gon' get these wings to grow.

   Refrain

2. Got people in de Promise Land,
   So gon' work until these wings expand.
   Don't care much 'bout flyin' high,
   But feelin' safe to land.

   Refrain

3. When I see that star up in de sky,
   I know de place that I'm gon' fly.
   Once these wings lift me high,
   I'll go straight to de Promise Land.

   Refrain

18TH CENTURY DAYDREAM

I bet we got our own nation
by then and language, ways
of talkin' and dancin' and
shakin' hands

We gon' talk 'bout all we did
that day, what we traded,
how much we made while
sippin' sweet black tea on de
porch waitin' for de kitchen
lady to tell us to come on and
eat and we gon' hold a finger
up 'cus we only come when
we ready

The police gon' work for us
'cus we pay them real good
and if a thief come try to steal
our stuff imma call 'em and
they gon' come runnin' to lock
him up sayin' *ma'am I'm so
sorry for the ruckus*

I bet them white folks be
scared to cross our street 'cus
we dont let 'em up on our side
of town, so they gon' be
bangin' on our door askin' if

they children can learn in the
school we put ours in 'cus our
kin can do math and spell and
read better than theys can

When you look at pictures of
the government it's gon' be a
bunch of us sittin' and smilin'
and makin' laws 'cus we built
this country up from nothin' at
all

People gon' see that we so
pretty and gon' be layin' out
in the sun just tryna get a little
bit of the color we already got
a bunch of

But we gon' laugh and tell
'em you can't even pay no
money to look like us, but they
gon' pay us anyway just to
walk in the room 'cus one day
soon

The world gon' respect black
folks like us

PASTOR WHO HAS NEVER OWNED A UTERUS GIVES A SERMON ON HOW TO BLEED

Awoken by a familiar stench
the first of seven days begun,

A strange fruit fallen from those legs
rotting under rays of morning sun,

Impurity peaks the second day
this fruit ripening in reverse,

All life forms from sacrifice
a body's pain becomes its worth,

Bleed private in this time
all is made unholy by one touch,

Pry the spirit free from skin
and bathe your soul above,

Herein must a choice be made
upon which salvation depends:

Wrap oneself in matrimony
conceive to repopulate the land,
                or
Face this fire until the grave
and on the death's first day,

Burn again.

ALL THINGS GO

In adolescence, the most magical part
was knowing a human and being
convinced she is transcendent.

These days, the most painful part
is being human and knowing
you had once been perceived as magic.

LIKE GOD

she convinced inconsequential beings
of their magnificence

she gave man consciousness then
watched him callously misplace credit

yet she is undeterred by this denial of her
for she knows she exists in their steps

sitting stagnant and stony in the past, aware
she consumes every piece of the present

this being is sustained by the
improbability of her existence

she is stoic to how you forget that
she painted a never-ending universe

then when finished, went back
and sculpted depth within it

she placed planets into nothingness

and from mystery

grew dimensions.

PART IV:
STOCKHOLM SYNDROME

want to ask Granny if Stockholm Syndrome requires consciousness, or if even a bug the size of our fingertip is entitled to food and a comfortable place to sleep. I would ask if she or the roaches is the captive between these four walls. I would tell her I think the roaches could leave the Southside sooner than her if they wanted.

Granny says: I forgot to ask Carl what he want for dinner.

My mother scoffs; pushes the full ashtray further away, and reminds us that she had her first and last cigarette at fourteen.

Mom says: The last time I saw a roach in my House, I hired an exterminator to come every week until I could feel them gone.

My Mother lies just like Granny; I have laid on a mattress filled with bedbugs long after my Mother felt the first bite. I notice how my Father recoils in response to her as a host would a parasite. His face contorted, confronted with how roaches define their co-residents. As if reminded of that phrase about being the company you keep. His wife's mere existence makes my Father not as clean, not as in control, not as different from other niggas as he had once believed. He lists external reasons for how his marriage got this way, infested. Maintaining that my Mother is patient zero, and he is the victim of her contagious disease. He does not conclude that he is likely just as unclean as she is.

For twenty-five years my Mother has taken his contempt head on like a soft breeze, wiping off indignation like dripping sweat, thinking deodorant will hide the fact that she still stinks. She placates my Father by trying not to agitate him, by treading lightly. As if stepping on roaches is an effective way to slow their spread. I don't know how she does it, I just know it could never be me.

I wonder how many years it took my Mother to internalize my Father's words, to start agreeing with everything he told her she was. When did she start pretending to be so different from Granny?

I suppose if Stockholm Syndrome is hereditary, the disorder varies its presentation enough to convince Black women that they are not

A PRINCESS SEARCHING FOR A SOULMATE

I do not want a *Listless* prince;
a spoiled boy with an open mouth who waits in place for rain,
the ones who lack that certain ache, that catalyst for change.
The necessary burning, that ceaseless hankering,
to rise from bed each morning, and grab all he can carry.

I do not want a prince who is *Easily Distracted*;
I have a feeling I am too high up and forgotten far too often.
If I fall from here my truest love must be waiting there for me
to break my fall, and most of all, to prevent my heart from shattering.

I do not want a prince who is much *Too Self-Important*;
who gives his claim before a query or contends to know of order.
Who infers the sky's decision, says all dark clouds will soon erupt,
who never expects a miracle, who forgets that I am one.

What I want is a prince who has his *Two Feet Planted;*
who intuits when to repot and can sense my roots expanding,
who builds for me space to grow, though stays as close as he can be.
I want to be attached to him while maintaining agency.

I want someone *Compassionate;*
who has felt a snowflake's frosty bite, who can empathize with
avalanche and understand the blizzard's plight,

I want to love a *Mindful* prince;
who does not speak in any tense, is apathetic to approaching seconds,
and prefers to love in moments.
or
someone from all those bedtime stories my mother read to me
of soldiers who cross shaky bridges and storm the dragon's keep.
Who brushes lips with one gentle kiss, and rescues me from hurt.
Can discern true love with just one glance,
so I wouldn't need to say a word.

TO TIWA

Have you ever seen a chameleon,
the way she melts into the tree?

The way she extends herself to a size
as big as any entity she meets?

How she sheds the skin she's in
just as easy as she breathes?

Or so any being she holds on to
could never feel that lonely?

One chameleon I know
fell in love with a worker bee.

He was young, and he was thirsty,
it was nectar that he needed.

She morphed her skin to echinacea,
opened her pink petals in the breeze.

Hoping that with time,
love would conquer fallacy.

She learned the truth of this world,
love might use you up then leave.

Once full, her lover flew away,
back home, to feed his only queen.

A JESUIT EDUCATION / FAITH FOR-PROFIT

The matriculants welcomed in mid-September
      Feature high chins and straightened spines,
Revel in the crass ornaments of elitist splendor
      As they parade directly under strangling vines.

Son of God is suspended above scholarly dread,
      As a polygraph pinned upon each passageway,
Scanning the classroom in search of pure reverence,
      Discerning the souls truly suited for accolades.

Arms outstretched and perpetually in sacrifice
      While Ignatians search for His Father in all things,
Christ inspects lecture halls for a proper paradigm
      Not paid for in Cash or Ego or Ancestors' Dreams.

Jesus lifts hung head to ask, *why are you here?*
      The Negro presents Him a wax-sealed acceptance,
Proud to share no likeness to Professor or Peer,
      This deviation serving as testament to his merit.

The Negro is awarded with coveted admission,
      Preference to those well distanced from their stock,
Jesuits enslaved them to fulfill a Godly obligation,
      Systemic philanthropy deems The Society absolved.

Scorned Messiah condemns this place of profit
      Justifying ungodly oppression in His Father's name,
Granting such empty acclaim without repentance,
      Who told The Negro to find reparation in this place?

Who told him that *this* is worth everything Jesus gave?
      Who told him that *everything* is worth Just This Much?

MOLECULES AND CELLS, 9:00-9:50 AM M|W|F

Professor draws Southside potholes made flush with
cancerous cells, says:

> when white blood don't attack
> the hood no more, black wealth
> might start to spread.

Professor shows a spectrum of light used up by chloroplasts, says:

> Bureaucracy absorbs war in
> red and blue—in blood and bruise—
> then reflects the green in (c)ash.

Professor speaks in laws, in conservation and mass, says:

> Consider fuel from a half-ashed cigarette conspiring
> with oxygen to sign a private prison's death certificate
> (in which ink is carbon dioxide, and the excess water is sent to Flint)
> in an exothermic reaction, the result is often dystopian.

Professor outlines life's conditions and calls it homeostasis, says:

> In achieving balance, bodies attack all foreign
> parasites and pathogens, but the gap between those two—
> between total health and sickness—holds
> crumbling cities, big-eyed children, and a settled fog
> that hides the rest.

Professor asks the class of equity, and how to achieve such a
state, says:

> The study of biology and molecules and cells attests that
> the smallest parts of this universe are governed by law
> and guided action.

Thus, when they challenge revolution, it is necessary to remind them—

The concept of human equity poses too complex a question,

to be addressed with code and canon or the same framework as the atom.

PUBLIC SWIMMING POOL (WHITE ONLY)

Freedom is a funny thing.
I am told I am quite lucky . . .

Do you see any bars in front of you?

There is no steel to stop me
from coming or going.

But when I escape,
might I find only water
at the horizon?

And standing on a precipice,
might I realize my body
has evolved to run
and not to swim?

PART V:
PLAYING TO LOSE

Granny's House sits on a one-way street off of 67th and Western, engulfed by the Southside of Chicago. It is glued together by staggered auburn bricks and features one square attic window beneath the peak of a pointed roof. Two patches of grass are shaded by red awnings. The rest of the yard is left a constant victim of the atmosphere. The most durable part of Granny's House is the Front Gate, ornamental and made of aluminum. Though once Black, the Gate is now a splotchy gray, consumed with a muted copper rust. From the street, there is no apparent entrance. Granny's House shows the world its profile, as if it was built to be ashamed.

To the far right of the grass, the Gate, closed and secured, stands before a cement path. Granny ensures the Gate is never left unlocked, even though it has already failed to keep the most persistent intruders out. A person could climb the Gate if they were so inclined or could pick the lock easily. Still, we must wait for Granny to waddle out holding a key in front of her chest. She allows us in and we follow the cement path to the House's face.

Granny's House has lived through seasons, surviving without choice on where it was placed or who would live between its walls, standing despite the trouble that constantly walks its sidewalk or bites at its stomach. Granny's House would tell you it did not want to be built on the Southside of Chicago, to become infested with roaches, or for residents who do not care about anything unattached to their blood or body. Most Houses hope to witness unconditional love, to hold onto art, to raise babies and puppies. A House has no choice but to stand out in the rain while someone occupies its body, so it must trust that whatever happens in its insides will not compromise its integrity. If it is lucky, its mortgage will be paid, but that is unlikely. A House cannot pack itself up and move to a place with less turmoil or uncertainty. It does not touch the other Houses sentenced to a similar fate, and can derive no comfort from shared condition or tribe. Granny's House must remain where it is planted, must accept its circumstance, must come to terms with the loss of a situational lottery, odds purposefully placed outside its favor.

A House like Granny's does not aspire to much other than survival.

Granny's House will endure, here, with Granny, for as long as she pleases, and will endure on, without her, once she leaves.

THAT LOT ON THE CORNER

They made that empty lot a corner store where my cousin bought diapers | the cashier stay behind plexiglass | the owner don't sound like us | he got stuck up over a pack of ramen | told to hand over everything he got | as he pleaded for his life to a man that ain't no god

They made it a church | pews was empty too many sundays in a row | the alderman already praise the corner over | new pastor got the tithes to make rent | but not enough for the benz he covets | so he forfeited his deposit | walked like moses through water | in search of a hustle that could buy him a whip

They made it a playground | never see kids there though | it's not safe alone | mama gotta *work like a dog day and night* | diapers too expensive on the other side of 5th | the territory was claimed by niggas who swing monkey bars | but don't play around

They don't fill that empty lot no more | it grew thick weeds that hold hands and birth sweet blackberries in summertime | like they got something we don't | twelve-year-old next door plucks and pops 'em | the way he seen big brother do at home

They bought all property next to the lot | dug a big hole | on sunday we prayed | for a place with a few jobs | some cheap milk maybe | a few weeks later | trucks passed by my house | dumped food scraps and plastic and human shit in the lot's gut | sucked out all its oxygen except for a little bit

They fill that empty lot on schedule now | the fumes make Big Mama's cough worse | we stopped breathing through the nose a while ago anyway | and kids ask too many questions | like | why my mama so pissed the alderman bought a place the town over | why we ain't seen his whip at the church ever since | my cousin robbed the corner store on 5th?

JAIL CELL WITH A BALCONY

the hood next to an airport
but escape from here ain't easy
march for rights, closed fist to sky
but rights ain't what babies eat

lil man sold dope, got 25, same
percent they tax it at dispensaries

untouched chitlins at Sunday dinner
a remnant stench of slavery

depression may wane in summertime
but bullets will fly more casually

mama likes a big bouquet
and the backyard got them free
so baby went out to pick her some
all he gave her was some weeds

rent a place to keep family safe
but wasteland live next door
seems all the bad left in this life
is lined thin with shiny silver

they say black wealth
can replace the pain but
even the price of pain too steep
and those that got it flex for profit
trade in they mama's dignity

♫ *fuck a greedy welfare Jezebel*
always asking for some money
don't fuck her, though, that easy hoe
these black bitches just not for me ♫

i swear something about this life
feel like a jail cell with a balcony

AFFIRMATIVE ACTION

If I could
use this skin to buy something
I'd buy so many other things
like the last two-fifths of your
seltzer like a suburban white
house with a picket fence in Naperville
or some place super-duper rich or like a black
therapist who like gets it like a last
name that my ancestors picked like a non-white
Jesus or even like
a Jesus that's mixed I'll take
anything like a religion not forced
on temple like a whole wardrobe
without any cotton in it whatsoever or like a ship to
sail back to a country of origin or like
legit anywhere else or like I don't know a time
machine to find some version of a great
america if that even exists
like seriously this list is
literally not exhaustive and seriously
if I could truly
use this black skin as currency there are like fifty
thousand trillion like
so many more things that would be so
much more fun to purchase than' some
crusty unseasoned seat at a university
you don't think I belong in.

TO JOSH

There are three plants in my home
I have chosen to love and care for

They ask for water every day
Even though I am trying to live, too

I notice their sadness at the poorest times
Like when I am late and rushing out the door

For a moment I will stop, stare at the drooping leaves
And in the time it would take to water them, ask:

Them or me?

DIVERGE

And if I do choose,
what of altered fate?

explain, then
what you have avoided.
what you have gained.

And if I choose neither,
what of fate altered?

explain, then
what have you gained?
what have you avoided?

PART VI:
A GUN WITH DEMENTIA

Granddaddy walks into the living room and ignores us, picks up a peppermint from the bowl next to my Mother, ashes his cigarette, and leaves to court another Kia at his favorite car dealership. The door closes behind him, we do not hear the lock click, only footsteps, the Gate screech open, bang closed, and the start of an engine.

Granny peeks through the shades and mentions how he's been more aggravated than he used to be, shorter temper than she remembers, how he never locks that Gate when he leaves. She said he's been smoking in the bed much more than he did when he started doing it about three years ago.

When Granddaddy returns, he goes straight to his bedroom, lays in the bed and chain smokes next to a loaded gun on the nightstand, puffing to the cadence of the television. Granny walks into the room,

> She says: Carl, you never lock that Gate when you leave this house and I'm sick of it.

Grandaddy picks up the gun and points the barrel to her chest.

> Granny screams: Carl imma call the cops if you don't stop it!

Granddaddy puts the gun down and leaves again. The lock does not click.

Granny puts her head in her hands. A roach runs toward me. I wonder what kind of hell it could possibly be escaping, what it must have experienced, to seek refuge in the very being praying for its extinction. Maybe it wants to die. Or maybe there is no point in assessing a roach's motivation because roaches are just stupid.

> Granny says: Kill it.

And I do.

3 FUNERALS

A brother
who held me close
since conception
linebacker-like stature
chooses couches &
controlled blue light
over turmoil live-action

I prefer when CGI
casually die
on my television

A street
claiming souls daily
salty-sour with bitterness
and swollen from lil man's
misplaced contempt is
caved in from neglect,
paved in by teddy bears
and candle wax from
pushers and soldiers

and brothers

I watch as his
potholes increase

A Cabrini-Green
walk-up
mayor call it a birthmark
on a city face, windy city
taxes pay to remove vanity
stains, no more metaphors
now for this drugged-up
ebony imperfection left
to lay like rubble in
the street for days

I smell death
while Daley dances,
city planning on all
three of them little
boys' graves

THANK YOU FOR YOUR SERVICE

american-born brother
will fight for white rights;
he will not cry over blue wounds
he will bleed out
he will stain his country red
      for tourniquet
he will not beg
he will regain consciousness
he will clean up his mess
he will sing
      My Chains Are Gone, I've Been Set Free
he will stand & place hand on chest
he will be granted the highest honor
he will be awarded poorer health
he will accept the sentence ruled
he will never pay off his debt
he will be asked to fight once more
      to this,
he will answer yes
he will salute to fifty stars
he will watch the stars wave back
      though for every star he follows North
he will know of freedom less
he will prove to Sam his loyalty
he will fly the broken flag
he will dream of rest once war is done
he will not be permitted that.

AFTER MYLES' MIRANDA

Did you ever stop to think
that the dark scares me,
too?

That I see
my reflection
and I scream

just like you?

WHISPER HER NAME

I been a dead body floating,
been sunken and suffocated
by heavy water, been motionless
have the media convinced
it's just a case of another black
woman who can't swim,
have the movement label
the coroner a bigot

Knowing full well

The exact moment I stopped
fighting, stopped pushing
against gravity in hope
the waves would baptize me,
drowned myself in an attempt
to rinse off the stench of
the self-fulfilling prophecy
wrapped like anchors around
my feet since the beginning

If I float myself to sleep
I pray to be reborn a martyr,
not apologetic for coveting
platitudes of the living or
for lying post-mortem

I have fought time
and time again to swim

I have found
the water's tension
oppressive

You haven't?

THE LUCKY ONES CAN REST AFTERWARDS

I notice my privilege
as I comfort myself
mid panic attack:

> *just wait*
> *twenty minutes*
> *then*
> *you can rest.*

PART VII:
ALL SIN AND SALVATION

Even though Granny got roaches, I still sleep over some nights. Usually on Saturdays because I like the way she moves knowing her morning will be holy. She holds onto hope that if I sleep next to her I will be more inclined to go to church the next day. She told me this in prayer once while we laid in bed under a portrait of White Jesus on a crucifix. Granny whispers sermon in my ear, telling White Jesus that if he would trade her sin for salvation she would be eternally faithful, pleading as if she is not both sinful and faithful already.

Granny ignores both of our burning souls in the same way she ignores the roaches running over White Jesus' lips while she prays.

The first man I have ever had faith in reminds me of Granny's Jesus. He makes me feel heavy, makes me feel euphoric, then makes me feel unworthy. Before him, I never believed in anything that was blind to my senses, but no matter how hard I try, I still cannot explain why I so intensely love this man, when to him, I can be so easily dismissed.

> Granny says: Son of God, please preserve my health and my grandbaby's innocence.

With eyes open wide as she speaks in scripture passages; I wonder if she knows I already gave it away to a few people I no longer speak with.

A LITTLE BOY MEETS RAIN AND THUNDER, PART 1

at the time, he was listening to daniel caesar real heavy,
said that he felt my soul in every melody
he said   *baby, listen to the lyrics carefully*
                 i notice how the rain and thunder follow you around
                 i think it's beautiful how sometimes your days be ugly

he said   *you remind me of how the sky golf claps when god*
                 cries
                 when i'm with you, i feel like the warm rain that used
                 to tap dance on my mother's thin roof at nighttime

he said   *you remind me of the lover i had hidden in my mind*
                 since age ten
                 when i'm with you, i know why real men don't buy
                 umbrellas
                 i'm a real man who stands against your heavy wind
                 i take you in and i am born again
he said that i was a tsunami drowning him, but for some reason
he could only see the rainbow at the end, the gold pot waiting for him,
he says that he is strong enough to withstand all of me and love me
harder . . .   even if i almost kill him.

A LITTLE BOY MEETS RAIN AND THUNDER, PART 2

watch big storms from window sills and imagine comforting the gods,
fantasize about forces of nature and the strength to pull them in,

> dream of a relationship symbiotic; of you, neither drowned by
> the weighted wet of rain nor made lost by the push of wind.

when big storms approach, anthropomorphize and name them,
though having never felt destruction up close,

> you still hear sirens and run for safety, you ain't ever been
> next to a levy that broke.

leave the house and its impediments, hybridize yourself with the
unknown,

> of course, I know just how far you will journey toward me,
> before returning home.

HOW TO LOVE

envision me completely naked, solely skin
and soma and last petal plucked from nucleus,
left with a *she loves me* and bare stem placed
on still river, a reflective plate of glass asking
you to see yourself seconds before forced into
a gravitational story *i'm sorry* I didn't know
how close we were to the edge,

touch me tender, as a feather's celestial slide
across harp, weaving itself through string like
matrimonial lace before consummation, virginal,
play a song across my spine, first from top to toe,
then left to right, construct a crucifix across my
anatomy to find any reason for sacrifice,

will you soak up my sins?

will you convince yourself

that I am Holy?

A LITTLE BOY MEETS RAIN AND THUNDER, FINAL PART

looking back, i can't believe i missed it, because big storms often
catch the attention of little boys watching hesitantly from window
sills, so when they decide to leave the house against their mama's
advice to go play for a minute with the big storm transfixing them,
those little boys only get to the sidewalk before being hit by wind's
right hook, and it isn't until concrete hits that little boys realize
the rain doesn't feel so pretty when you're in it but

this is that young love shit,

when we start to get real it dissolves to lust . . . shit

the problem with it was a few clear skies in summertime made him
jump too quick, so he was already free-falling when he checked
and saw his parachute was missing, because to little boys, maybe i
just shimmer like the rain they saw when they sat from afar,
maybe i am simply every big storm little boys' mamas tell them
to stay covered from, the dark clouds surrounded and he hit on
the pavement too hard, and our love wasn't love enough to make
the pain worth it, i mean . . . we had just started off, by the end i
figured every flood was my fault, he even told me so, and in the
next breath he said it wasn't me

said,   *maybe we didn't realize how different we are*
said,   *maybe we don't fit like we thought*

and i thought, if i had a time machine i would get in it, go back to
the start and tell god get rid of all my flaws, tell him to stop every
storm he had coming, and when god says he can do nothing, i'll
get back in the time machine and span the relationship, prolong
every moment so that i would not fall in love so quick, and when
the love becomes inevitable, i'll notice the moment the sky starts
to twist, confront hectic hurricane before she blows us back to

toxic, and if i can't win against her, we'll cross like five/six dimensions until we get to a remote location, watch me, i'll build a bunker to protect us from any cataclysm tryna stop me, we'll live in a private place where natural disasters sit dormant.

i'll pack up my flaws,

walk to the bottom of me and burn them in the basement with every match on the planet,

and in the case that they don't catch,

in the case that flames fall off flaws like raindrops roll off plastic,

in case dysfunction latches onto unions like storm clouds hug horizons,

in case conflict sinks into skin like tattoo ink,

in case suffering is permanent,

i'll open up the time machine and fill it with every imperfection and insecurity, stow lighting strikes behind snowflakes, patch every levy begging for relief, i'll send them far into the future so that you can only see the best of me,

so this time,

you will *actually* fall in love with me,

. . . and decades will pass,

my imperfections collecting dust,
we'll be gray-haired & wrinkled by the time they catch up with us,
and when the moment arrives . . .
when my flaws wash ashore . . .
when we're at last face-to-face with those big storms that broke

us before,
i'll open up the time machine finally convinced i have fixed it,
convinced we can weather any storm approaching in the distance,
and when you *still* fuck me over you lowdown,
dirty,
coward,
piece of shit,
i will get in my time machine,
travel to that little boy at his windowsill,
i will reach past every part of myself that I hid from you in there,
offer to your mother my most sincerest of condolences,
i will pull out Armageddon and Extinction, and ask for your choice.

FAIRY GODMOTHER'S TWO CENTS

When a child pretends the dried glue on her palms is peeling skin
We laugh, knowing vital pieces of ourselves do not detach so easily

The Princess views her heart as a home with chipping paint, and
Love picking a scab and hoping the wound reheals a better way

A Damsel unable to extricate Distress from her identity
Exists in decay until prince charming offers up a remedy

The Princess desires revival, healing, and to begin again anew
A world consumed with survival leaves little room for rescue

Although she understands the harmony between character and cape
And of the skill required to care for her and handle all the ache

To be self-aware is not merely an awareness of oneself
To know of love is cerebral while knowing love is felt

She remembers being told of those endowed with the ability to save
Figures to love herself and heal she must request external help

It seems that being so much aware,
                    might leave you with far too little self.

PART VIII:
TO FEAR NO PURGATORY

Now that I stay up later, I watch her more closely. Regardless of her pain, and regardless of her innocence, Granny truly moves as though she is Holy. Bonnet secured on her head, one Marlboro behind each ear, slippers on feet, and no teeth in her mouth since it's past ten. I see her differently ever since I have been allowed to stay up past seven-thirty.

All of those years, she never went to Granddaddy after she tucked me in. Instead, she'd retreat to a room behind the kitchen that holds dusty boxes of unused Raid and value packs of cigarettes stacked one on top of the other. I plop down in a plastic lawn chair and notice how Granny's chest strains to rise with each inhale.

Granny says: Baby, what about your asthma?

I say: I've been around cigarettes before.

Granny shrugs and places the filter in the ashtray. Roaches must be godless, must fear no purgatory or apocalypse, existing without truly knowing death. Roaches recognize neither God nor his prodigy, so for them, it does not matter whether Jesus is White or Black. And maybe that's it; perhaps that's the difference between a roach and a person. We worry about what will happen to us at the end of all this, but for roaches an end will never come.

Granny lights another cigarette. Sometimes it feels like she is trying to suffocate the roaches. Maybe she thinks choking herself, too, is the only way. Granny should know roaches do not die easily, and by the time one does, it has already made ten more in its place. It's strange; none of the roaches that torment Granny today were the first ones to break into her House. Only two, now long dead, needed to get past the Gate in order for Granny to be in the situation she is now.

As Granny lights her third, the House begins to look as if each cigarette butt she finishes grows legs, and doesn't stop walking until Granny gets dizzy tracking each upside down on the ceiling. Every time she chain-smokes a new part of the house is painted in polka dots. I think it turns them on; the roaches make babies under the warm cover of nicotine.

WHEN WEEDS TURN

a volatile being
metamorphosis

yellow lion-tooth petals
do as they please.

praying for

these weeds turn
coveted textile
in july

at the center of life
and root of profit
a contradictory form.

to resemble
snowball

defined
without it
name
closed

by drastic change
yet addressed
even though
and opened again.

and alien
by the same
they have

i envy them
desiring
unwrapped
off.

how i am glued together
that gentle grip on self
waiting for novelty

this way
light
to be carried

i am known
flightless
to die this way.

before cocoon
ground-dependent

inhibited
and believed

i am attached
to comfort
are not.

to order
though these

arrangement
lesser beings

we place
durability
bonds

so much value
the permanence
but,

in the
of these

if we are rope
by strand
hook
from ourselves

if we stretch
tension will concentrate
and when we snap
change manner

break strand
on a final
separate
we will

dissociate and become unfamiliar to each other
as well.

too often we wrap ourselves in origin
for safety for each other.

no chance to debut ourselves again.
how little faith in love
must we have to hold on as we do?

how scared of each other
we must be to lie about rebirth,

to tire of our first selves yet still
stitch them into now,

attempting to remain in bloom forever.

MEDUSA SPEAKS OF A STONE

You are petrified already; shivering under time's ephemeral weight; your end is inevitable; you cannot avoid a change in state.

You beg for life; cower before a hissing choir, at the prospect of being frozen; fearing a changing metric of time; your world is defined by the cadence of a singular muscle; proven time after time to inevitably lose its rhythm, allowing the life it holds to rot, become void, still; consciousness rescinded; your entire self governed by the certainty of death, apocalypse, extinction.

Serpent-crowned woman does not find demise in her creations; she strengthens ailing flesh; implores a skeleton to stand more strain, to be split down the center, to not expire as consequence; multiplying, instead, as a rough-edged and freckled anchor who can respond to any name; who feels the warm palms, the gentle rotation, that one open eye, zooming in close; who retains its soul through phases.

She has known a precious stone; not merely those carved by her gaze; structures birthed from core to crust; prehistoric caves and homes of hieroglyphs; ground zero to the bodies of ancient beings, their outlines, a tattoo engraved on its face; meccas of history and evolution; irreplaceable tools; wielded weapons; long roads cracked from winter salt and places to go; shaved and polished gift shop trinkets; foundations reposed under skyscrapers, decades spent supporting a foreign aesthetic.

She has not known a sculptor; who asks of all a rock has been before chisel; of fiery magma spilling from a volcano's lips; how it turns cold, solid, igneous; then granite; pulverized by human hands; divorced from the condition preceding it; still alive, even if contrary to the form fate intended.

You are petrified already; shivering under time's ephemeral weight; your end is inevitable; why not choose your change in state?

THE ORIGIN OF EBONICS, PART 2

this new language as a tongue removed from body,
as mother's muted call from a distant room,

or as traveling leaves, fallen from primordial limbs,
carried far away then gathered into a dense embrace

of strangers, all dying & detached like we are,
formerly our own, now reduced, concentrated into one,

negro miseducation as hot needle stitching
secular in full verse on displaced throats,

as illiterates weaving season's bloom into currency,
perspiring over stove & field, but never calculating wage,

this new sound is a guttural smoker's cough,
stained lungs adapting to colony elocution

& this temporary staccato respiration used
as evidence of surrender, of servility,

as a rationale to brand the raised hand
inquiring of pen or alphabet or definition

POLARIS

Plantation born, a woman of natural stench,
Does not take off her shoes in my house, does not sit.
Grazes my skin with bare hands, a migrating herd on new grass . . .

I wear this privilege with a hunched spine,
In need of a direction not illuminated under starlight.
My fate not immobilized by deep pigment, illiteracy, or bondage . . .

She said she seen me in a daydream once—
I was a clean rag soaking perspiration from upper lip.
The vibrational hum sending shivers down a textile stem.
Warm water nudging suds' passage from breast to thigh.
Gravity enforcing its ethic of feet planted,
        and the ground pushing back, insisting on flight.
She said she ain't know that stars could die.
Believed death's approach to always be evident,
        witnessed naked after excess blood or in gasping breath.
She said *then you must be them seven minutes.*
The peace between what's known and what's next.
Ignorance so blissful it is only labeled the latter.
Periods that follow sentences. An evident start and its end.
She said *you ever had to ask a question?*
How strange it is to meet a statement, a proclamation.
A black body not clothed in the world's condemnation.
Lacking the fear of that nebulous time in between.
Devoid of the constant anticipation of inevitable grief.
She said it made sense why my voice is so foreign.
She raises my chin. Inquires why it points to the ground
        when I am the wish she placed on every shooting star,
        with her head always tilted up, towards the clouds.
She is happy how different we are,
        she always prayed we would be strangers upon meeting.

YOU, A THEIST

Krishna and Buddha and Shiva and Nameless,
no human-held pen has written one correct.

These Gods reject a mortal's image.

You, a theist, should know that.

Instead,
praise the vacuum   the pictureless
the populated   praise the earth
praise the infinity   the generational memory
the zero   praise the empty womb
praise the mega   the multiverse
the microscopic   praise the atom.

Address single-digit senses
abandon fiery worlds under feet
perceive pearly gates simplistic
approach this sacred world with piety.

Those who uncover the ant's altruism
who relate to parasite before deity
may learn the matriarch's mental map
may lead journeys far longer than
the trail after Nazareth.

Seek the promise of Eternal Bliss
to cross its threshold by any means
but do not forget, salvation also exists
mixed amongst the soil and stars and sea.

The Wholeness you pursue is far closer than you think and is
waiting to be sculpted by the heaven surrounding you in pieces.

Look! *Look.*
Holy is here already.

PART IX:
ASSESSING CAPTIVITY

If nicotine gave Granny order, if it offered her some sanity, if she needed to find companionship between those four walls and the roaches provided her with company, then *ignorance* would not be the right word to describe Granny's survival. Ignorance could not explain how she avoided succumbing to the surface tension that has suffocated so many others. Granny cannot be ignorant of the ocean if after decades she has yet to sink, must have mastered the water long ago to still be safe and treading. There is a high chance her survival is intricately linked to White Jesus' presence, to her unrelenting belief in Him.

Placing faithlessness central to my identity used to cement for me the notion that I was poles apart from Granny. I would never live in a home with roaches or let my husband treat me like a pew at the church. Only recently has it become easier to admit there are parts of myself I have yet to find. To entertain the theory that I have been tainted since conception, and scrubbing my body raw will not be enough to cure me if infected. I have learned why roaches enjoy the warm busyness of an attic; it is often a safer place to hide and packed densely enough to nest. Perhaps starting there will allow me to unravel how to properly assess all of the other realities I have recently been uncovering within myself.

I do not own a house yet, but when that time comes, it will not always be clean. Comfort often turns into addiction, swallowing those who least expect it. I am also devoted to a man who cannot love me back and pine after what imprisons me. As dust piles itself on ledges and concentrates under couches, the dirtier my House gets, the easier it will become to marry the promise of a pure Heaven, even if uttered by a man who has no qualms with my current captivity.

Right now I suppose my body is the only home I own and, like Granny, I have terror tucked away in its basement. There are spaces in my psyche I figured were piled too high to safely excavate, so I sequestered boxes in the back of an unswept attic thinking my past could be tucked far enough away. The only result is a woman inaccessible to herself, a hostage hidden beneath a hoard, hoping the faith she desires might be found somewhere among the unemancipated parts of her.

IT IS CALLED SOUL FOOD

because it has a duality that is rare to find:

This force not only sustains life,

but is also a reason

to stay alive.

DYSMORPHIA

Dysmorphia rests on the surface of a sun visor's vanity mirror, on silent walks past dark storefronts, at least five camera rolls, in Gianna's sunglasses and above the bathroom sink,

Dysmorphia ignores the reflection's depth, the hairline fracture peep-holes, overlaid on mirror image, does not notice those eyes, staring at you, those voices, begging for freedom, those fists, banging on the back of glass,

Dysmorphia conceals your other forms;
        The Empath   The Anarchist   The Abolitionist
unnoticed fractions of you laid separate, of one heart and dissenting, unanimous, willful, all birds, caged behind steel bars, clamoring in discordant song,

Dysmorphia has not met these others;
        The Chameleon   The Optimist   The Protagonist
living behind this fractured glass, the ones who open their eyes each sunrise, shake their heads, *no*, with feet planted, fighting for life, back of head to top of back, eyes closed and howling,

So the next quiet evening Dysmorphia appears, over the bathroom sink or front camera, close your eyes, listen for the riot rising behind your reflection,

Wait, wait,

The Warrior will break free,

Acknowledge them, tell them about the war of dawn,

Tell them to return tomorrow, ready to fight.

EMOTIONAL BY DESIGN

Does the Earth ask for change to halt?
To not know of winter's bite?
Does it prefer a certain state of being,
and to stay that way through time?

Or does the Earth beg for seasons?
Does it welcome cleanse and shift?
Does it dream of reincarnation,
and becoming new again?

Has the Earth not made the answer clear?
Not used your breath as evidence?

That constant change produces life.

That constant sun will kill it.

PERHAPS ALONE . . . BUT LONELY?

I walked down the street holding nothing's hand, felt
nothing reach between valleys and felt nothing hold on tight

    when I said, "I am just like you,"
    nothing pressed on my chest,
    knocked me into cold concrete,
    and we laughed, 'cus I felt *something*
    like pain and pump and bone . . .

I had dinner with zero in silence, eyes locked for hours
over empty plates, deep secrets exchanged telepathically

    when I asked, "what are we?"
    the diners around us vanished,
    we became as blank as beginning,
    every new second of silence
    a color adding onto us . . .

I laid next to absence again as birds welcomed new sun,
we used their harmony to compose a song on the ceiling

    when I whispered, "I love you,"
    absence shrunk to my silhouette,
    or I expanded myself into it,
    and we became whole, together.

LIKE THE BIG BANG

despite her evidence, she is caged and questioned
despite impatience, she quietly waited

allowing time and space to fall perfectly into place
before she made suns under pressure

despite fatigue, she awoke blowing stardust
from her fingertips to illuminate any darkness

and despite distinction sprinkled life like rain
not caring what it looked like or on which part it landed

despite inexperience, she consulted no one
remaining quiet until she exploded

conjuring magic so complex that billions of years later
even *white men* have yet to understand it

despite insistence, she took her time growing
she started as a singularity and spread to the cosmos

she reached the ends of the universe

and kept on going

PART X:
MY INHERITANCE

Granny asks why I only like white boys.

She says: Your mama shouldn't have put you in that school.

I laugh and tell Granny she's confused; I am more like her than she realizes. This time, I don't mention White Jesus. We both deserve to know an all-encompassing love, even if we differ in how we believe that looks. Granny must find my lack of faith, and my inability to extend my devotion outside of my senses to be unconscionable as well. In the end, love doesn't need a reason to be what it is.

As I am starting to understand Granny's struggle a little better, I have been reassessing some things. If I find traits in my Mother that look like the ones in Granny, I know there must be traits in both of them that can be also found in me. All three of us have experimented with different means of pausing misery, and have prayed to not be shamed for our mistakes. After all, we are the ones best suited to help abolish each others' pain.

To understand what a roach is to a House, consider what a Black woman is to patriarchy. One bug never seems like a problem. But before you can catch it, your soul is infested, and an exterminator can't help if you don't have any money. When you know how it feels to be an intruder in a place you have built with bare hands, maybe it is easier to give the first roach you see something to eat.

On the chance that Stockholm Syndrome is abnormal, that it should be diagnosed and treated, I could accept that this affinity I feel towards a man who cannot love me is partially hereditary. What is more clear, though, is that these devotions my Mother and Granny and I hold so close, this unending affection consuming us . . . proves the extreme depth, the full-blooded ability we possess to give a similar, equally boundless type of love to ourselves.

THREE-FIFTHS

if an entity will be called on,
if it will claim the space it sits

there can never be a void,
where a void itself exists.

THE ORIGIN OF AFRICAN-AMERICAN VERNACULAR ENGLISH

yet   under burnt ash
embers spar with assimilation
like how middle earth & crust swallow debris
but spin on. blazing core black lungs grip
oxygen & echo the anguished chorus,
that lullaby sung when bated & bald
& just begun living. this altered cry,
a hybrid soprano pitch, a sore-throated nod
to freedom, a vernacular cypher of revolution
& future weapon. a hit held in & passed again.
spun on & passed again, clockwise,
through generations.

BEEN A LOT MORE

I been alive before
let summer sunlight dry my tears before
let echoes fly my voice to places I never been
let my toes be painted rainbow colors and chased it
I been a pot of gold before

lifted planetary weight, I been had to hold myself up
let time take away the pain, been patient, been tough
been too much and just enough, healed a broken
woman with just one touch, I been a God before

been flawed, been tsunami, been hurricane and lightning rod
been in an empty room and still heard audience applause before

I seen bones unbreak before, I been unbreakable before
been brave | been the choir | the pastor | pew | the next page |
I been the newest testament before
been saved even never having seen a cape before
been loc'd | been loaded | been natural | been noticed
how every time I dive deep oceans I been floated
been the next wave | been soaring | been coasting

I apologized and meant it, I changed ways before

been in wars that made me tougher
been mourned my lost lovers

been caressing all my scars with shea butter . . .
        and I seen every single one of them fade before

ARE CREATION

black women are creation
the mother of everything that exists

you poke holes in her womb
not realizing you bloom within it

but when she has had
enough of your torment

when her patience wears thin,
maybe she will walk away

maybe her love will end
maybe this time

she will let you
be born into darkness

and maybe this time

she will refuse
to breathe light into it.

WHAT WAS THE POINT OF ALL THIS?

I am learning the value
of my body, of my voice as
a seasonal change, a slowly
curated work of art, an ode
to a future her.

I refuse to tie her up
in whole or happy ending;
the last time I placed
shiny bows on misery,
I healed,
then mistook deferred
pain for gift and
had to start again.

I hope in excavating
purposefully to core,
I may fill her with
tears and teeth and time,
yet never reach brim.

At the end of this,
I hope to carry the heavy
in light stride and reject
the pretty, shallow dent
I used to remedy sorrow in.

ABOUT THE AUTHOR

Miya Coleman is a performance poet born and raised in Chicago, IL. Miya first discovered her passion for poetry in 2012 during a middle school poetry slam. Since then she has performed around Boston and Chicago. Most notably, for Congresswoman Ayanna Pressley and the Congressional Black Caucus, at Harvard University, as well as being crowned champion of the 2021 Roxbury Poetry Festival. Coleman is eager to focus on the uniquely human experiences that connect us all despite harrowing realities. Having recently completed her Masters in Applied Development and Educational Psychology as a Double Eagle at Boston College, Miya hopes to use poetry to uncover the psychological and cultural roots of who we are, and who we have the power to become.

BOOK RECOMMENDATIONS FROM THE AUTHOR

Still Can't Do My Daughter's Hair by William Evans

This collection by William Evans tells the story of trauma and change through an appreciation of specific, singular memories. The poet weaves us through past and present by situating the reader square in a focused moment of time and placing it like a puzzle piece in the broader story. The beauty of this collection is the intentionality of wielding those seemingly mundane conversations, actions, moments, and asking the reader to give them weight, to give them respect. Evans does not summarize perspective or process, but rather suggests that to uncover growth one must focus on those instances where it truly lies; tucked inside the smallest pieces of everyday life. I am left wondering how my view of the world has been influenced by one comment, one movement, one action. I am left wondering about the singular moment which made it clear that who I am now is vastly different from the person I once was.

Ain't Never Not Been Black by Javon Johnson

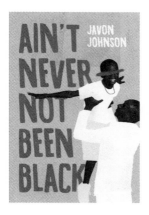

In this collection, Javon Johnson offers perspective on the Black experience from all angles. There is no sugar-coating or hand-holding; there is only a raw and uncomfortable truth that the reader must digest and breathe through. It takes a personal, specific Black experience and situates it into the all-encompassing Black experience felt by many. Johnson allows the reader to relate to common wisdom and, at the same time, uncover novel thoughts and emotions. This collection uses a variety of form and length, humor and grief, personal and collective, to take the reader on a journey of unapologetic Blackness.

OTHER BOOKS BY BUTTON POETRY

If you enjoyed this book, please consider checking out some of our others, below. Readers like you allow us to keep broadcasting and publishing. Thank you!

Michael Lee, *The Only Worlds We Know*
Raych Jackson, *Even the Saints Audition*
Brenna Twohy, *Swallowtail*
Porsha Olayiwola, *i shimmer sometimes, too*
Jared Singer, *Forgive Yourself These Tiny Acts of Self-Destruction*
Adam Falkner, *The Willies*
George Abraham, *Birthright*
Omar Holmon, *We Were All Someone Else Yesterday*
Rachel Wiley, *Fat Girl Finishing School*
Bianca Phipps, *crown noble*
Natasha T. Miller, *Butcher*
Kevin Kantor, *Please Come Off-Book*
Ollie Schminkey, *Dead Dad Jokes*
Reagan Myers, *Afterwards*
L.E. Bowman, *What I Learned From the Trees*
Patrick Roche, *A Socially Acceptable Breakdown*
Rachel Wiley, *Revenge Body*
Ebony Stewart, *BloodFresh*
Ebony Stewart, *Home.Girl.Hood.*
Kyle Tran Mhyre, *Not A Lot of Reasons to Sing, but Enough*
Steven Willis, *A Peculiar People*
Topaz Winters, *So, Stranger*
Darius Simpson, *Never Catch Me*
Blythe Baird, *Sweet, Young, & Worried*
Siaara Freeman, *Urbanshee*
Robert Wood Lynn, *How to Maintain Eye Contact*
Junious 'Jay' Ward, *Composition*
Usman Hameedi, *Staying Right Here*
Sierra DeMulder, *Ephemera*
Taylor Mali, *Poetry By Chance*
Matt Coonan, *Toy Gun*
Matt Mason, *Rock Stars*
Sean Patrick Mulroy, *Hated for the Gods*
Rudy Francisco, *Excuse Me As I Kiss The Sky*

Available at buttonpoetry.com/shop and more!

BUTTON POETRY BEST SELLERS

Neil Hilborn, *Our Numbered Days*
Hanif Abdurraqib, *The Crown Ain't Worth Much*
Sabrina Benaim, *Depression & Other Magic Tricks*
Rudy Francisco, *Helium*
Rachel Wiley, *Nothing Is Okay*
Neil Hilborn, *The Future*
Phil Kaye, *Date & Time*
Andrea Gibson, *Lord of the Butterflies*
Blythe Baird, *If My Body Could Speak*
Andrea Gibson, *You Better Be Lightning*

Available at buttonpoetry.com/shop and more!